ULTIMATE CHARACTER GUIDE

SO CUTE

By Jenne Simon

SCHOLASTIC INC.

Pikmi Pops! What's inside? Pikmi Pops! A cute surprise!

All rights reserved. Published by Scholastic Inc., *Publishers since 1920.* SCHOLASTIC and associated logos are trademarks and/or registered trademarks of Scholastic Inc.

The publisher does not have any control over and does not assume any responsibility for author or third-party websites or their content.

ISBN 978-1-338-31605-6

10 9 8 7 6 5 4 3 2 1   18 19 20 21 22

Printed in the U.S.A.   40

First printing 2018

Book design by Becky James

Welcome to the world of Pikmi Pops,

where little pops hide big surprises! Inside every pop is an adorable animal who can't wait to meet you. These adorable animals and cuddly creatures can be soft, fluffy, or sparkly, and always smell as sweet as they look.

Find out more about Pichi the Dog, Gizmit the Guinea Pig, Fetti the Cat, and all their furry friends in this ultimate guide to the Pikmis. Whether you're chasing rainbows with Fancy the Unicorn, monkeying around with Leroy the Monkey, or just hanging out with Selby the Sloth, as long as you've got a Pikmi by your side, you'll follow your nose to adventure.

SWEET

SO CUTE

Pichi

SO CUTE

If someone is feeling blue, Pichi does whatever it takes to make them laugh. That is want makes Pichi such a doggone good friend.

Animal: Dog
Season: 1
Rarity: Rare
Scent: Blueberry
Known for: Digging for blueberry bones

Dream Vacation: New Yorkie City
Favorite Snack: Blueberry bones
Quote: "Don't worry. Be yappy!"

4

Ollie

Ollie is a lover, not a fighter. Ollie is in love with love and always tries to help friends find furr-ever happiness!

Animal: Bear
Season: 1
Rarity: Rare
Scent: Bubblegum
Twin: Sorbae
Known for: Having a lot of heart

Favorite Day: Valentine's Day
Quote: "I'll always be bear for you!"

Picki

Picki the Parrot is a high flier who loves performing acrobatics. Risky and rad, this bird attracts a crowd. There's always a surprise or two in the show!

Animal: Parrot
Season: 1
Rarity: Common
Scent: Fruit Paradise
Personality: A total tweet-heart

Likes: Tropical breezes
Dream Vacation: Hawaiian luau
Known for: Creating new fruit juice combos

Fetti

SWEET

A colorful kitty who's always merry when eating raspberries. Fetti leaves ripe red pawprints all over the place.

Animal: Cat
Season: 1
Rarity: Rare
Scent: Ripe Raspberries
Hobby: Picking Raspberries!

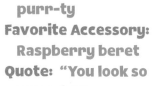

Known for: Looking purr-ty
Favorite Accessory: Raspberry beret
Quote: "You look so purr-ty!"

Ebby

Ebby the Bunny can bounce around like a bubble! Ebby just has to be careful not to pop and end up in a sticky situation!

Animal: Bunny

Season: 1

Rarity: Rare

Scent: Bubblegum

Nickname: Sir Bounce-a-lot

Hobby: Bubble Juggling

Plays: Basketball

Quote: "You're a bun of fun."

SURPRISE!

Leroy

SO CUTE

This monkey loves bananas so much, Leroy's starting to become one! However, Leroy's scent is very a*peel*ing!

Animal: Monkey
Season: 1
Rarity: Rare
Scent: Banana
Known for: Banana skin skating

Prized Possession: Yellow slippers
Favorite Snack: Banana flavored *anything*
Quote: "You're the pick of the bunch."

Wubbs

Everything is upside down in Wubbs's hangout! But that's okay—it's always so dark in there, Wubbs never knows which way is up anyway!

Animal: Bat
Season: 1
Rarity: Common
Scent: Caramel
Hero: Dracula
Favorite Snack: Caramel tacos

Believes in: Love at first bite
Quote: "Let's hang out together!"

Guggles

Guggles the Clown Fish is always surprising the Pikmis and making them laugh! If they don't laugh at Guggles's jokes, then it's time for a tickle attack!

Animal: Clown fish
Season: 1
Rarity: Rare

Scent: Grape Giggles
Hobby: Clowning around
Favorite Color: Purple
Sweet Ride: Clown car
Quote: "Always remember, any fins possible!"

SO CUTE

The smiliest shark you will ever meet, Voom makes friends fast. How could anyone resist a grin like that? Always quick with a joke, Voom has a sharp wit and even sharper teeth!

Animal: Shark
Season: 1
Rarity: Rare
Scent: Mint Choc Chip
Hobby: Surprising swimmers with a smile

Favorite Snack: Mint-choc-chip cupcakes
Dream Vacation: Finland
Quote: "You're looking sharp today!"

Squirl

SURPRISE!

Squirl the Caterpillar is always hungry. It's amazing what this Pikmi can do with a bowl of blueberries! Squirl's cocoon is one of the most popular restaurants in Pikmi Land. It's called the Berry Hungry Caterpillar!

Animal: Caterpillar
Season: 1
Rarity: Rare
Scent: Blueberry
Best Sport: Swimming, especially the butterfly stroke

Favorite Dance: Jitterbug
Prized Possession: Its cocoon
Sleeps in: Silk pajamas

Mooli

Mooli the Crab is full of silliness and has the softest claws you will ever feel! These arms are made for hugging, not pinching!

Animal: Crab
Season: 1
Rarity: Common
Scent: Watermelon
Known for: Being a snappy dresser
Hobby: Building sandcastles

Favorite Snack: Watermelon Popsicles
Sweet Ride: Taxi crab

Toogy

Toogy loves chasing anything that moves and sniffing out chocolate. This little pup always helps to chip in when there's chocolate to be found!

Animal: Puppy
Season: 1
Rarity: Common
Scent: Choc Chip
Hero: Cocoa Chanel
Dream Job: Pup star
Dream Vacation: Mocha Raton, Florida

Quote: "You're a total pup star!"

BE HAPPY

Juju

SO CUTE

Juju the Giraffe is a risk taker who sticks its neck out for friends. The other Pikmis always look up to Juju for inspiration!

Animal: Giraffe
Season: 1
Rarity: Common
Scent: Caramel
Nickname: Your Highness
Favorite Sport: Basketball

Hero: Tall McCartney
Dislikes: Giraffic accidents

Tickles

Tickles the Octopus can high-five eight friends at the same time—which is lucky, because Tickles is a *berry* popular octopus!

Animal: Octopus

Season: 1

Rarity: Common

Scent: Ripe Raspberries

Hobby: Arm wrestling eight Pikmis at a time

Sweet Ride: Fish tank

Sleeps in: A waterbed

Quote: "Legs be best friends!"

14

Bubbles

Bubbles is a *fin*tastically talented Pikmi. This fish can blow bubbles and juggle at the same time. It's one tricky underwater trick!

Animal: Goldfish
Season: 1
Rarity: Common
Scent: Bubblegum
Hobby: Taking bubble baths
Star Sign: Aquarius
Dream Job: Emergency room sturgeon

Favorite Movie: *Finding Nemo*

SWEET

Mumpy

Super-friendly Mumpy can hear besties coming from miles away! Always up for a hug, this bunny loves to wrap its ears around you!

Animal: Bunny
Season: 1
Rarity: Common
Scent: Vanilla Bean Marshmallow
Favorite Music: Hip-hop

Prized Possession: Hare brush
Quote: "You are music to my ears!"

Middy

SWEET

You will only ever see Middy after dark! Middy hosts the best slumber parties and is always the last one to fall asleep.

Animal: Owl
Season: 1
Rarity: Common
Scent: Watermelon
Hero: Harry *Hoot*dini
Hobby: Stargazing

Favorite Subject:
*Owl*gebra
Quote: "You're *hootiful*."

Moosh

Moosh the Kitten loves highland dancing. Moosh has the fastest-moving paws in the land!

Animal: Kitten
Season: 1
Rarity: Common
Scent: Vanilla Bean
    Marshmallow
Known for: Playing
    hopscotch

Favorite Play: Cats
Favorite Team: Carolina
    Panthers
Sweet Ride: Catillac

SURPRISE!

Numble

When Numble is not snoozing, this bear is jumping out from trees to give surprise hugs! Numble's squeezes are designed to please!

Animal: **Bear**
Season: **1**
Rarity: **Common**
Scent: **Caramel**
Favorite Movie: *Sleeping Beauty*
Hero: **Teddy Roosevelt**

Dream Vacation: **Sleeping Bear Dunes, Michigan**
Quote: **"I can't bear being without you!"**

SO CUTE

Hobnob

Hobnob is one helpful hamster. Happy to bend over backward for friends, Hobnob also loves to have fun and go a little crazy!

Animal: **Hamster**
Season: **1**
Rarity: **Rare**
Scent: **Mint Banana**
Hobby: **Practicing the hamster dance**
Dream Job: *Rodentist*
Likes: **Fairy tails**

Dislikes: **Dumbbells**

Ooky

Ooky's a cheeky little thing who loves to swing and surprise you by popping bubblegum bubbles when you least expect it!

Animal: Monkey
Season: 1
Rarity: Common
Scent: Watermelon
Known for: Listening to "POP" music!

Dislikes: Pitching a fit
Favorite Music: Pop songs
Quote: "You're the tops when it comes to pops!"

Kaz

This Pikmi's head is always full of fresh ideas to make life more fun! Kaz lives in the only watermelon tree in Pikmi Land. It's a great place for a growing imagination!

Animal: Squirrel
Season: 1
Rarity: Common
Scent: Watermelon
Personality: Nutty
Best Friend: A unicorn
Favorite Color: Pink

Quote: "You're one in a melon!"

SO CUTE

Tumbles

Tumbles loves to bark and woof! Running, jumping, and tumbling all around the garden is just so much fun!

Animal: Puppy
Season: 1
Rarity: Super set
Favorite Snack: Pupperoni pizza
Signature Dance Move: The tail wagger
Favorite Play: *Hello, Doggie!*

Best Joke: What happened when the puppy went to the flea circus? He stole the show!

Miska

SO CUTE

SWEET

The coolest kitten in town, Miska loves hanging out with Tumbles! Sweet like raspberries, Miska loves chasing pieces of string and reflections on the wall.

Animal: Kitten
Season: 1
Rarity: Super set
Favorite Fairy Tale: *The Little* Purr*maid*
Dislikes: Making *meow*ntains out of molehills

Best Joke: What do you call a kitten with eight legs who likes the ocean? An octo*puss*!
Quote: "You're *meow*velous!"

Hoodoo

A born comedian, Hoodoo makes everyone laugh. A tree-swinging giggle factory, when Hoodoo starts cracking up, all the Pikmis follow!

Animal: Monkey
Season: 1
Rarity: Super set
Prized Possession: Monkey wrench
Favorite Snack: Bubblegum banana sundaes

Sweet Ride: *Furrari*
Quote: "You're a barrel of fun!"

Tambo

Tambo has wings, but this parrot prefers flying by bubblegum balloon instead. This beaming bird catches everyone's eye as it floats by!

Animal: Parrot
Season: 1
Rarity: Super set
Hero: Robin Hood
Hobby: Parrot-oke
Favorite Song: "I Believe I Can Fly"
Quote: "Some birdie loves you!"

Naz

A bear who's always there, Naz has a heart of gold and never complains. Naz is always ready to assist Fez in one of Fez's magic tricks!

Animal: Bear
Season: 1
Rarity: Super set
Hero: Yogi Berra
Favorite Snack:
 Honeycomb
 marshmallows

Dislikes: Grizzly movies
Best Joke: What did the
 teddy bear say after
 dinner? I'm stuffed!

SO CUTE

Fez

Trickin' 'n' prankin' is what Fez does best! Full of surprises, Fez is always popping out of top hats and disappearing without a trace.

Animal: Bunny
Season: 1
Rarity: Super set
Prized Possession: Top hat
Best Trick: The
 disappearing rabbit

Favorite Game: Hopscotch
Quote: "It's time to shine."

Pingle

SWEET

Pingle the Hedgehog really sticks out from the crowd! Shy but super sweet, Pingle rolls up into a ball when anyone pops by.

Animal: Hedgehog
Season: 1
Rarity: Ultra rare
Scent: Caramel
Known for: *Hedgehugs*
Hobby: Playing pinball

Hero: *Quill*iam Shakespeare
Quote: Sending hedge-hugs and kisses!

SO CUTE

Ickle

Ickle loves to talk and squawk and has a good word for everyone! This little parrot even talks in its sleep. If you have a message to send, this is the bird to call!

Animal: Parakeet
Season: 1
Rarity: Rare
Scent: Grape Giggles
Known for: Fly style

Hobby: Talking, talking, and talking!
Likes: Talk shows
Quote: "You're the squawk of the town!"

SURPRISE!

Selby

BE HAPPY

Selby the Sloth has plenty of time for everyone. Pikmis rush to get in line for one of Selby's hugs, which last for ages. It's certainly worth the wait!

Animal: Sloth
Season: 1
Rarity: Common
Scent: Blueberry
Known for: Hanging around

Hobby: Racing snails
Sweet Ride: Slowmobile
Quote: "You're slow amazing!"

Gizmit

SO CUTE

SWEET

Like a mini lawn mower, Gizmit the Guinea Pig is always hunting around for the sweetest grass to eat! Come over for lunch one day and share a *hay*burger.

Animal: Guinea pig
Season: 1
Rarity: Common
Scent: Caramel
Favorite Fairy Tale: *The Three Little Guinea Pigs*

Dislikes: Tests
Best Joke: What do you call a guinea pig who hates to fly? A groundhog!
Quote: "You're a real *squeak*heart!"

Flit

Flit the Butterfly is attracted to anything shiny and pretty and gets into a flap searching for gifts for friends! When this butterfly flutters by, it's a sign that you're in for a treat!

Animal: Butterfly
Season: 1
Rarity: Limited edition
Favorite Subject:
   *Moth*matics
Dream Job: Monarch

Likes: Gardens
Quote: "You make my heart flutter!"

Akwa

Akwa the Narwhal makes magic happen! This Pikmi loves blowing bubbles and then popping them with its horn. It's the best fun you can have with gum!

Animal: Narwhal
Season: 1
Rarity: Limited edition
Known for: Narly adventures
Hobby: Hanging out with unicorns
Dislikes: Tooting its own horn

Quote: "Narwhal always love you!"

SO CUTE

 Wawa

BE HAPPY

Wawa the Seal loves to swim and shake in every sea, river, and lake! If Wawa is your friend, consider that a seal of approval!

Animal: Seal
Season: 1
Rarity: Limited edition
Favorite Subject: Art! Art! Art! Art!

Likes: Swimming with friends
Favorite Color: Aqua
Dream Job: Navy SEAL

Folly

SO CUTE

SURPRISE!

Folly the Bunny's home is always a *hop*pening place! With *berry* long ears that are perfect to listen to the latest Pikmi Pop tunes, Folly is a bunny with *ears* of experience behind it!

Animal: Bunny

Season: 1

Rarity: Ultra rare

Scent: Blueberry

Likes: Listening to others' secrets

Dislikes: Those who don't carrot all

Best Joke: What did the bunny say to the carrot? It's been nice gnawing you!

Quote: "You're the bunniest person I know."

Neno

Neno the Owl is wiser than most, with an answer to any question. It may not be the *right* answer, but at least it will give you a giggle!

Animal: Owl
Season: 1
Rarity: Ultra rare
Scent: Banana
Favorite TV Show:
America's Got Talon

Believes in: Claw and order
Favorite Game: Trivial
Pur*shoot*
Quote: "Owl never let you down!"

Dollop

SWEET

Dollop always looks like the cat that got the cream.
This kitty always has its tartan handkerchief to keep
its whiskers clean.

Animal: Kitten
Season: 1
Rarity: Ultra rare
Scent: Grape Giggles
Dream Vacation:
　Glas*meow*, Scotland

Wants to Visit:
　Westminster Tabby
Likes: Playing the bagpipes
Quote: "You're the cream
　of the crop!"

Tuku

Tuku the Penguin always feels cold, and the best way to keep warm is a big hug! That's why you'll always find this Pikmi snuggling with friends.

Animal: Penguin
Season: 1
Rarity: Ultra rare
Scent: Blueberry
Hobby: Painting with
    watercolors

Dream Job: Hockey player
Prized Posession: Tuxedo
Quote: "Have an ice day!"

Bibble

SO CUTE

Bibble is one of the most thoughtful Pikmis. This little lamb uses its own wool to knit beautiful creations. Giving gifts is the *baaast!*

Animal: Lamb

Season: 1

Rarity: Ultra rare

Scent: Vanilla Bean Marshmallow

Dream Vacation: Hiking the Hima*lamb*yas

Personality: Gentle and sheepish

Sweet Ride: *Lamb*orghini

Quote: "You are woolly wonderful!"

Cloppy

BE HAPPY

Cloppy the Pony gives rides to other Pikmis when they are tired. They hold on tight to Cloppy's ears because it's always a surprisingly bumpy ride!

Animal: Pony
Season: 1
Rarity: Common
Scent: Fruit Paradise
Favorite Sport: Stable tennis

Dislikes: Charley horses
Favorite Color: *Neigh*vy blue
Quote: "You're the pony one for me."

SWEET

Chata

BE HAPPY

Chata the Parrot is always on the phone talking to friends. If you want the gossip going around Pikmi Land, just ask Chata.

Animal: Parrot
Season: 1
Rarity: Rare
Scent: Ripe Raspberries
Dream Vacation: The Canary Islands

Known for: Talking, chatting, speaking, and having conversations!
Dislikes: *Cheep* souvenirs
Dream Job: Diamond mynah

Tiki

SO CUTE

Tiki the Cow is a smooth *moooo*ver and loves to shake it up on the dance floor! When the music's finished, it's time to serve up some after-party grape milkshakes.

Animal: Cow
Season: 1
Rarity: Common
Scent: Grape Giggles
Star Sign: Taurus
Hangout: The *calf*eteria

Favorite Play: The Sound of *Moosic*
Dream Vacation: *Udder* space
Plays: Cowbell

SURPRISE!

Smorey

SO CUTE

Smorey has a heart for art! This creative pup is always surprising friends by making sweet art from the tastiest treats. It's art that's good enough to eat!

Animal: Dog
Season: 1
Rarity: Rare
Scent: Vanilla Bean Marshmallow
Hero: Pablo *Pawcasso*

Dream Vacation: The A-maltese Coast
Favorite Snack: Vanilla marshmallow sundae
Quote: "You're pawsome."

Kimie

Kimie is a cool cat who's a sweet treat to be with! Choc-full of love to share, this cat is the purr-fect pop to pick!

Animal: **Cat**
Season: **1**
Rarity: **Common**
Scent: **Mint Choc Chip**
Favorite Musician:
    Meowry J. Blige
Dream Job: *Purramedic*
Favorite Subject: *Hisstory*
Best Joke: **Why are cats good at video games? They have nine lives!**

Beeps

Beeps gives a hoot about the planet. Beeps conserves energy and *owl*ways recycles!

Animal: Owl
Season: 1
Rarity: Common
Scent: Banana
Favorite Movie: *Beak to the Future*
Likes: Reading joke books
Best Joke: What do you call a wet baby owl? A moist *owl*ette!

Quote: "You're a hoot to be with."

Squeaks

SWEET

With a sparkling personality, Squeaks the Mouse comes out at night to brighten up everyone in sight. Squeaks is a little mouse who's a big star!

Animal: Mouse
Season: 1
Rarity: Rare
Scent: Choc Chip
Known for: Karaoke
   competitions

Biggest Fear: Catfish
Wishes for: A
   *mouse*tache
Quote: "Gimme a squeak!"

Asha

Asha has ups and downs like everyone else. When you need someone to talk to, Asha is the one to pick—this bunny is always all ears!

Animal: Bunny
Season: 1
Rarity: Common
Scent: Peppermint
Known for: Hip-hop dancing

Dream Job: Hare Force pilot
Favorite Movie: *The Fast and the Furriest*
Prized Possession: Bunny slippers

Alfalfa

SO CUTE

Alfalfa sprouts happiness everywhere! This Pikmi scatters rainbow sprinkles in the garden beds and hopes that one day they'll grow into rainbows!

Animal: Bear
Season: 2
Rarity: Common
Scent: Watermelon
Hobby: Talking to its plants

Favorite Color: Green
Dream Vacation: Brussels, Belgium
Favorite Treat: Watermelon waffles

Loofa

With Loofa's designer coat and luxurious mane, this lion has its paws on the pulse of the latest trends!

Animal: Lion
Season: 2
Rarity: Super set
Hobby: Shopping on Mane Street
Favorite Treat: Roasted chickpeas

Favorite Movie: *The Lion King*
Happy Place: In front of a roaring fire

SURPRISE!

Kimchi

SO CUTE

Kind and super friendly, Kimchi goes out on a limb to help and *panda* to all your needs. You'll never feel blue with this red panda!

Animal: Red Panda
Season: 2
Rarity: Super set
Usual Breakfast:
  *Panda*cakes

Likes: Doing good deeds!
Favorite Toy: Fire engine
Favorite Color: Scarlet red

SWEET

Plume

Plume is proud to display stunning feathers—and why not? They're awesome! But Plume is no show pony . . . more like a show peacock!

Animal: Peacock
Season: 2
Rarity: Super set
Likes: Bright colors
Dislikes: Bird brains
Favorite Snack: Peanuts, green peas, and pecans

Favorite Pastime: Feather arranging

SO CUTE

Zeni

Zeni is not your average zebra. But then again, nobody is average in Pikmi Land! Zeni is a trendsetter who can't wait to hit the catwalk with a wild new look!

Animal: Zebra
Season: 2
Rarity: Super set
Dream Vacation: Africa
Dream Job: Referee
Favorite Treat: Pikmi Popsicles
Favorite Pastime: Styling up new looks
Best Joke: What's black and white and black and white? A zebra doing a flip!
Quote: "Stripes are so last season."

Skooter

BE HAPPY

SO CUTE

Skooter has a huge sweet tooth. A sugar rush helps this Pikmi glide through life with ease!

Animal: Flying Squirrel
Season: 2
Rarity: Super set
Nickname: Sweetie Pie
Known for: Flying by the seat of its pants
Dream Job: Pilot

Favorite Treat: Sugarcoated sugar cubes
Favorite Pastime: Kite flying

Puffly

SO CUTE

SWEET

If you need comfort, Puffly is the pug to call. This Pikmi will take friends for a walk to play in the park or give them a puggly hug!

Animal: Pug

Season: 2

Rarity: Super set

Likes: Puppy love

Favorite Food: Pugs in a blanket

Best Yoga Pose: Downward dog

Favorite Fairy Tale: *The Three Little Pugs*

Favorite Treat: Jelly Bean Jaffles

Favorite Pastime: Relaxing in a pair of fluffy Pugg boots

Bamboo

SO CUTE

Bamboo is one ultra-rare bear! Once you find Bamboo, you have a friend for life. You couldn't BEAR to lose a sweet Pikmi like this!

Animal: Panda bear
Season: 2
Rarity: Ultra rare
Favorite Game: Playing hide-and-seek
Hangs Around: The li*beary*

Favorite Treat: Bamboo steam buns
Dream Vacation: China
Scent: Caramel Apple

Dainty

BE HAPPY

Everyone knows that Dainty is light on its hooves. This donkey loves to get out on the dance floor and boogie to the beat!

Animal: Donkey
Season: 2
Rarity: Ultra rare
Scent: Blueberry
Known for: Shaking a tail
Favorite Treat: Hay enchiladas

Secret Pleasure: Tea parties
Favorite Musician: Bray-Z
Favorite Pastime: Giving donkey dance lessons

SWEET

Posie

BE HAPPY

Posie is a whole bunch of fun and loves performing for friends by juggling grapes. Posie's skills are so amazing, some Pikmis have even called it the "Grapest Show on Earth!"

Animal: Dog
Season: 2
Rarity: Ultra rare
Scent: Grape
Nickname: The Great Posini
Hero: Santa Paws

Hobby: Putting on *puppet* shows
Favorite Game: The Puppy Bowl

Bobble

Bobble loves talking. This budgie can chirp in five different languages, which is very handy when it goes migrating to warmer countries in winter.

Animal: Budgie

Season: 2

Rarity: Rare

Scent: Banana

Hobby: Spending time on Twitter

Favorite Movie: *Bye Bye Birdie*

Favorite Game: Duck, duck, goose

Favorite Treat: Banana-flavored birdseed

Quote: "Home, tweet home!"

Smoosh

This Pikmi has a "home, sweet home" on its back! No matter where Smoosh goes, there is always a beautiful place to stay. It's like being on an endless vacation!

Animal: Sea turtle
Season: 2
Rarity: Rare
Scent: Bubblegum
Super Skill: Interior decorating. You should see inside Smoosh's shell!

Favorite Game: The shelling bee
Favorite Accessory: Tortoiseshell glasses
Favorite Treat: Banana cream pie
Likes to Wear: Turtlenecks

Moni

Moni has an incredible memory! This elephant can remember everything it has ever eaten for lunch since it was one day old! Actually, it's not *that* remarkable, because Moni only ever eats raspberries!

Animal: Elephant

Season: 2

Rarity: Rare

Scent: Watermelon

Prized Possession: Trunk full of mementos

Favorite Play: *Elephantom of the Opera*

Favorite Color: Gray

Favorite Treat: Raspberries, and lots of them

Quote: "I will always remember you!"

Favorite Pastime: Playing memory games

Scoots

Scoots is a whiz in the water. This Pikmi is an expert swimmer—its backstroke is *otter*ly amazing!

Animal: Sea otter
Season: 2
Rarity: Rare
Scent: Watermelon
Hobby: Boating and body surfing
Dream Vacation: Tropical cruise

Favorite Treat: Bubblegum soda
Quote: "I *otter*ly love you!"

SO CUTE

Clove

Clove is an adventurous coyote who's always prowling around the plains looking for colorful things to create for friends. Clove really knows how to turn trash into treasure!

Animal: Coyote
Season: 2
Rarity: Rare
Scent: Banana
Nickname: Night Howl
Known for: Baking desert desserts
Favorite Treat: Moon cakes

Quote: "Your destiny is written in the stars!"

Velvet

SO CUTE

BE HAPPY

Velvet dreams of traveling through space. They say this Pikmi's antlers can pick up signals from other planets!

Animal: Elk
Season: 2
Rarity: Rare
Scent: Bubblegum
Closest Family: Its antler and uncle

Favorite Subject: Astronomy
Favorite Treat: Bubblegum tacos
Prized Possession: Telescope

Chomp

SO CUTE

BE HAPPY

Chomp has a small roar, but a big heart. This Pikmi doesn't need to be king of the jungle—it would rather be the *pawfect* friend!

Animal: Lion
Season: 2
Rarity: Common
Scent: Fruit Paradise
Hobby: Lion around in the shade

Dream Vacation: Safari on the Serengeti
Favorite Team: Chicago Cubs
Favorite Treat: Fruit salad subs

Fab

BE HAPPY

Fab's **fluffy** ears make for a great listener. This pup can always hear friends calling. And when Fab barks, it's truly from the heart!

Animal: Cocker Spaniel
Season: 2
Rarity: Common
Scent: Watermelon
Known for: Common scents
Favorite Play: *Fiddler on the Woof*

Favorite Weather: Dog days of summer
Favorite Treat: Watermelon sausages
Quote: "Fur what it's worth, I love you!"

SWEET

Snowy

SWEET

Snowy adores the cold weather and is always singing and dancing when there's a blizzard. This cool bear is famous for performing on the ice stage. This Pikmi loves being in "*snow*biz"!

Animal: Polar bear
Season: 2
Rarity: Common
Scent: Caramel Apple
Known for: Being totally chill

Favorite Treat: Caramel apple icy pops
Favorite Game: Freeze tag
Favorite Pastime: Singing in the snow
Quote: "You're so cool!"

Eggnog

SO CUTE

Whether Eggnog is faced with a complicated problem or just a tough nut to crack, this squirrel never gives up! Eggnog is very handy with power tools, especially jackhammers!

Animal: Squirrel
Season: 2
Rarity: Common
Scent: Grape
Dream Vacation: Black Forest
Favorite Pastime: Making cool jewelry from nut cases

Favorite Treat: Peanut butter and grape sandwiches
Quote: "I'm totally nuts about you!"

SURPRISE!

Skittle

SWEET

Skittle is always calm and will do anything for anyone. This llama is all about peace and likes to give advice about life to others. Some Pikmis call Skittle the "Dalai Llama"!

Animal: Llama
Season: 2
Rarity: Common
Scent: Cotton Candy
Dream Vacation: The Andes mountains
Favorite Treat: Cotton candy cornflakes

Favorite Pastime: Meditating under the cotton candy tree
Quote: "I'm your no-drama llama!"

SO CUTE

Glama

SO CUTE

SWEET

Glama the Peacock is always putting on a show and loves giving fashion advice to the other Pikmis. Glama's motto is: Be proud of yourself!

Animal: Peacock
Season: 2
Rarity: Common
Scent: Blueberry
Hangout Spot: The Chic Beak Salon
Favorite Color: Peacock blue

Favorite Pastime: Showing off great style
Dislikes: Ruffling feathers
Best Joke: What do you get when you cross a peacock and a porcupine? A sharp dresser!

Rowie

SO CUTE

If you spot something red in Pikmi Land, it's probably Rowie the Red Panda. Popping up in the most unexpected places to surprise you, Rowie is always red-red-ready to make you jump!

Animal: Red panda
Season: 2
Rarity: Common
Scent: Fruit Paradise
Hobby: Planning surprise parties

Favorite Song: "Row, Row, Row Your Boat"
Best Friend: Eggnog the Squirrel
Quote: "You *red* my mind!"

BE HAPPY

Puff

SURPRISE!

Puff knits adorable sweaters using a special soft wool. This ram has a list of orders for woolly cute creations that's as long as its horns!

Animal: Ram
Season: 2
Rarity: Common
Scent: Caramel Apple
Dream Vacation: Bucking-ram Palace

Reads: *The Wool Street Journal*
Likes: Counting sheep
Plays: French horn
Favorite Treat: Caramel apple cupcakes

Tickle

Tickle has sensitive hooves. Even a single blade of grass can make it fall over in a giggling fit! That's why Tickle is the only zebra who likes to wear socks.

Animal: Zebra
Season: 2
Rarity: Common
Scent: Blueberry
Always Wears: Socks
Likes: Laughing and giggling
Favorite Color: Black and white

Favorite Treat: Blueberry hay bales

Tubble

Tubble is sure-footed on the dance floor and sure-eatin' at the dessert table. This goat can't resist a sweet treat!

Animal: Goat
Season: 2
Rarity: Common
Scent: Cotton Candy
Nickname: Greatest of All Time
Dream Vacation: The mountains
Favorite Artist: Vincent Van Goat

Favorite Treat: Cotton candy and tin cans
Best Joke: What do you call a goat who knows martial arts? A karate kid!

SO CUTE

Pickle

Pickle the Pug's tail never stops wagging! A happy pug who loves to have a bunch of fun with friends, Pickle is a grape buddy to everyone!

Animal: Pug
Season: 2
Rarity: Common
Scent: Grape
Dream Job: Barkaeologist
Plays: The trombone
Favorite Treat: A big bunch of bones

Favorite Pastime: Walks in the park
Best Joke: Why do pugs hate the rain? They don't want to step in a poodle!

Wisp

SO CUTE

Wisp is a mythical Pikmi who flies down from the mountains to spread the message of friendship. Those special enough to see Wisp know that they have a friend for life!

Animal: Dragon
Season: 2
Rarity: Limited edition
Nickname: Flame
Known for: Getting fired up

Hobby: Skywriting with fiery breath
Super Skill: *Talon*ted fire-breather
Favorite Treat: Anything hot and spicy

Fuzz

BE HAPPY

Fuzz feels most chilly playing in the snow. This yeti may look cold, but the truth is, it's extra warmhearted!

Animal: Yeti
Season: 2
Rarity: Limited edition
Personality: Cool as a cucumber
Hobby: Building snowmen

Favorite Treat: Snow cones
Quote: "You're snow amazing!"

SO CUTE

Fancy

SWEET

Like a rainbow, Fancy appears when you're least expecting it. Then, just as quickly, Fancy disappears again! So be sure to make a wish—fast!

Animal: Unicorn
Season: 2
Rarity: Limited edition
Favorite Color: Rainbow glitter
Super Skill: Making magic happen

Favorite Accessory: Golden horn
Favorite Treat: Rainbow Cake
Favorite Pastime: Rainbow sliding
Quote: "I believe in you!"

Flubb

When Flubb has a new passion, watch out! This Pikmi can be so pumped up that it's practically bursting with excitement!

Animal: Pufferfish
Season: 2
Rarity: Ultra rare
Scent: Banana
Hobby: Making balloon animals
Dream Vacation: Scuba diving
Biggest Flaw: Inflated ego

Favorite Game: Basketball
Favorite Treat: Banana bubblegum

Noodles

Noodles gets spooked easily. But when this sea creature gets a case of the wobbles, it takes a deep-sea breath and keeps on swimming!

Animal: Jellyfish
Season: 2
Rarity: Ultra rare
Scent: Bubblegum
Best Friend: Its i-tentacle twin
Favorite Treat: Jelly, of course!
Favorite Pastime: Rock-pool hopping

Dislikes: Fishing for compliments
Sweet Ride: The Octobus

Tubbs

SWEET

Tubbs is never unhappy and is always having a whale of a time! This Pikmi loves to spout about how much fun Pikmi Land is to anyone who will listen!

Animal: Whale

Season: 2

Rarity: Ultra rare

Scent: Watermelon

Nickname: Squirt

Hobby: Deep-sea diving

Dislikes: Blubbering

Favorite Treat: Fish and chips

Kazoo

SO CUTE

Kazoo is a real joker and quacks everybody up with lots of silly antics. And if they don't laugh, Kazoo tickles them with a feather! Everyone's lucky to know this ducky!

Animal: Duck
Season: 2
Rarity: Rare
Scent: Chocolate
Speaks: Portu*geese*
Hero: Billy the Kid
Favorite Treat: Chocolate

Favorite Pastime: Taking baths
Best Joke: What do you call a bird with fangs? Count Duckula!

Dreya

SO CUTE

SURPRISE!

A little rascal who loves to pull a prank, that's Dreya! Watch out when this raccoon is out and about, because you never know when it might surprise you with a trick up its sleeve!

Animal: Raccoon
Season: 2
Rarity: Rare
Scent: Grape
Known for: Planning the best prank
Favorite Treat: Raccoon macaroons

Likes: Stealing attention
Best Joke: Why do raccoons sleep under cars? They like to wake up oily!

Oni

Playful and silly, Oni loves splashing around in water and getting others wet. Sometimes naughty, but always nice in the end, this otter can be a lotta trouble!

Animal: Otter
Season: 2
Rarity: Rare
Scent: Bubblegum
Dream Job: Making change at the river bank
Hero: Harry Otter
Known for: Getting along swimmingly with others
Sweet Ride: *Otter*mobile

Favorite Treat: Orange ice cream
Favorite Pastime: Floating and boating

Fuwa

Fuwa the Fox is very tricky. You'll see this Pikmi Pop's tail popping over the hills—but catching it is a different story!

Animal: Fox
Season: 2
Rarity: Rare
Scent: Raspberry
Personality: Sly
Known for: Telling tails
Favorite Team: Boston Red Fox
Favorite Dance: The fox-trot

Favorite Treat: Lemonade lollipops

SO CUTE

Mani has an amazing imagination and never stops creating fun inventions for the other Pikmis. Mani's job is to put a smile on everyone's face—and this moose does it so well!

Animal: Moose
Season: 2
Rarity: Rare
Scent: Mint Choc Chip
Dislikes: *Moose*quito bites
Favorite Sport: Track and Field

Likes: Mooseical theater
Dream Vacation: Alaska
Favorite Treat: Choc mint *moos*li
Favorite Pastime: Growing organic food

SWEET

Fluff

Look up in the trees and you may find Fluff the Koala. Fluff loves to sleep all day long and party under the stars! No one loves nature more than Fluff.

Animal: Koala
Season: 2
Rarity: Rare
Scent: Caramel Apple
Known for: Tree-hugging

Dream Vacation: Australia
Favorite Treat: Caramel-coated gum leaves
Favorite Drink: Coca Koala

SO CUTE

Nacho

BE HAPPY

Nacho may be small, but this bulldog has a big personality. Confident and clever, you are always in good paws with Nacho!

Animal: French Bulldog
Season: 2
Rarity: Common
Scent: Caramel Apple
Dream Vacation: Paris
Favorite Dance: Ballet

Favorite Treat: Candy apple cornflakes
Favorite Pastime: Learning to bark in French
Quote: "I dig you!"

Tazzle

Energetic and adventurous, Tazzle loves surprising friends by pouncing out from the jungle. This Pikmi is a little tiger who loves playing tag until the sun goes down!

Animal: Tiger
Season: 2
Rarity: Common
Scent: Fruit Paradise
Favorite Accessory: Striped sweater
Biggest Flaw: Being a copycat
Favorite Song: "Jungle Bells"

Hero: Tigger
Favorite Treat: Mango marshmallows

Niblet

Niblet is a totally *ham*azing friend! This Pikmi also has a need for speed. Niblet loves to feel the wheel beneath its feet!

Animal: Hamster
Season: 2
Rarity: Common
Scent: Mint Choc Chip
Hero: Abra*hamster* Lincoln
Dream Vacation: Hamster-dam
Favorite Game: Hide-and-squeak

Favorite Treat: Choc-dipped carrots
Quote: "Have a *ham*azing day!"

SO CUTE

Twigs

Twigs is a real copycat! Ever since learning to talk, Twigs repeats everything it hears. This Pikmi chats 24-7, including while it's asleep!

Animal: Parakeet
Season: 2
Rarity: Common
Scent: Chocolate
Hero: Tweety Bird
Dislikes: Feeling caged in
Favorite Color: Yellow
Favorite Movie: *Lord of the Wings*
Favorite Treat: Apple seeds

Favorite Pastime:
Listening to talk radio

Freckle

Freckle has a real sweet tusk, so it always remembers to brush twice a day to keep its smile sparkling!

Animal: Walrus
Season: 2
Rarity: Common
Scent: Cotton Candy
Hobby: Beach volleyball
Hangout: The dive-in movie theater
Prized Possession: Polaroid camera

Favorite Treat: Cotton candy-crumbed fish

SO CUTE

Snaffle

SWEET

Snaffle can remember every Pikmi's name and address, which is very handy when writing Christmas cards!

Animal: Elephant
Season: 2
Rarity: Common
Scent: Raspberry
Hero: Cinderellephant
Dream Vacation: India

Waiting for: The Tusk Fairy
Favorite Play: *Stomp!*
Favorite Treat: Strawberry and peanut ice cream

Erkle

SO CUTE

Erkle the Turtle is a shy little Pikmi who doesn't like to come out of its shell. Everything Erkle needs is on its back. But once this shy Pikmi decides to poke its head out, the fun really begins!

Animal: Turtle
Season: 2
Rarity: Common
Scent: Banana
Hobby: Watching *shell*evision

Dream Job: Ninja
Favorite Treat: Peaches and cream
Sweet Ride: Shellicopter
Quote: "Let's shell-ebrate!"

Brite

BE HAPPY

Brite is a very handy friend to have around on a rainy day. This Pikmi's antlers are perfect for hanging wet socks out to dry!

Animal: Deer
Season: 2
Rarity: Common
Scent: Blueberry
Hobby: Ballroom prancing
Likes: Sledding

Favorite Month: December
Favorite Weather: Rainy days
Favorite Treat: Pumpkin pie

SWEET

Petrie

SO CUTE

Petrie likes to decorate by hanging bunches of grapes from the ceiling. That makes it much easier to have a midnight snack without getting out of bed!

Animal: Wolf
Season: 2
Rarity: Common
Scent: Grape
Believes in: _Furr_ever friends

Favorite Song: "Blue Moon"
Favorite Treat: Grape jelly
Quote: "You're _howl_arious!"

Peebie

By day, you'll find Peebie taking a catnap in the sun. But by night, it's on the prowl for adventure!

Animal: Cat
Season: 2
Rarity: Common
Scent: Bubblegum
Hero: The Pink Panther
Dream Vacation:
   *Meow*nich, Germany

Likes: Beating im*paw*ssible odds
Dislikes: Sourpusses

Rhubarb

Rhubarb is a smart roo and doesn't stop thinking about the future. This Pikmi carries watermelon seeds in its pouch and plants them wherever it goes! That way, Rhubarb can have watermelon anytime, anywhere!

Animal: Kangaroo
Season: 2
Rarity: Common
Scent: Watermelon
Hobby: Boomerang juggling
Favorite Color: Watermelon Pink
Favorite Treat: Watermelon waffles

Prized Possession: Boomerang
Quote: "I couldn't be hoppier with you!"

Tater

SWEET

Tater loves looking for treasure in the yard. This Pikmi spends hours digging holes and is always on the hunt for those rare banana bones.

Animal: Golden Retriever
Season: 2
Rarity: Common
Scent: Banana
Known for: Its doggie paddle

Hobby: Drawing treasure maps
Favorite Treat: Banana bones
Dislikes: Barking up the wrong tree

Parfait

Parfait the Hedgehog eats nothing but desserts! But don't worry—this hedgehog makes sure to get its daily vegetable intake. You should try Parfait's recipe for broccoli cream pie!

Animal: Hedgehog
Season: 2 PushMi Ups!
Rarity: Ultra rare
Scent: Choc Swirl
Personality: Layered
Known for: Being a ball of energy

Favorite Treat: Chocolate-coated carrots
Favorite Pastime: Cooking up new creations in the kitchen
Nickname: Spike

SURPRISE!

Sprinkle

SO CUTE

Sprinkle is a little sweetie. And when it's bouncing off the walls, its favorite marshmallows make sure it's always in for a soft landing!

Animal: Hamster
Season: 2 PushMi Ups!
Rarity: Ultra rare
Scent: Marshmallow Treat
Known for: Its big mouth
Dream Vacation: New
Hamstershire

Favorite Treat:
Marshmallow muffins
Favorite Flower: Rodent-
dendron
Favorite Pastime:
Workouts in the hamster
wheel

Drips

Drips the Dog is a sweet but messy pup! Always getting into sticky situations, Drips melts the hearts of everyone by leaving chocolate heart-shaped pawprints behind!

Animal: Dog
Season: 2 PushMi Ups!
Rarity: Rare
Scent: Chocolate Ripple
Known for: Checking its collar ID
Hobby: Paw printmaking
Favorite Treat: Chocolate ripple cake

Favorite Color: Chocolate brown

Sherbet

Sherbet the Parrot is a bit of a daredevil and likes doing tricks through the clouds. Sherbet always carries a bubblegum bubble to ensure a soft bouncy landing!

Animal: Parrot
Season: 2 PushMi Ups!
Rarity: Rare
Scent: Marshmallow Treat
Known for: Having *soar* muscles
Hobby: Sending messages on Flapchat
Best Trick: Flying with one wing tied behind its back

Favorite Music: Squawk n' roll
Favorite Treat: Bubblegum birdseed

Sundae

Sundae the Cow can whip up the creamiest sundaes using the freshest ingredients. Sundae has all the dance *mooo*ves to make that ice cream extra smooth!

Animal: Cow
Season: 2 PushMi Ups!
Rarity: Rare
Scent: Berry Twist
Known for: Telling a*moo*sing stories
Favorite Dance: The banana split
Plays: The cowbell

Favorite Treat: Berry twist dundaes
Quote: "Pretty please, with a cherry on top?"

Sweetie

Sweetie the Goldfish loves meeting new friends, but can never remember their names. That's okay, because Sweetie gets to introduce itself all over again the next day!

Animal: Goldfish
Season: 2 PushMi Ups!
Rarity: Rare
Scent: Very Berry
Known for: Swimming laps
Favorite Color: Gold
Favorite Team: Los Angeles Lakers

Favorite Treat: Berrilicious fish food
Favorite Pastime: Doing laps of the fish bowl

SO CUTE

Ripple

Ripple thinks bubbles are a-meow-zing. It loves to watch the purr-fect spheres float through the air!

Animal: Cat
Season: 2 PushMi Ups!
Rarity: Common
Scent: Bubblegum Ripple
Known for: Chewing bubblegum
Favorite Musician: Kitty Perry
Dislikes: Bursting anyone's bubble

Favorite Team: Detroit Lions
Favorite Treat: Bubblegum ripple cake
Favorite Pastime: Bubblegum baseball

Twirl

Twirl spends all its time picking berries and pulling pranks. Things get *berry* messy when it's around!

Animal: Monkey
Season: 2 PushMi Ups!
Rarity: Common
Scent: Berry Bliss
Known for: Monkeying around
Favorite Movie: *Planet of the Apes*
Favorite Color: Blue
Favorite Treat: Berry surprise pie

Favorite Pastime: Swinging in the berry bushes
Sweet Ride: Chimp Blimp

Puddin

SWEET

SO CUTE

Puddin is a real show pony. It loves to perform daring leaps and sweet twirls in front of a crowd!

Animal: Pony
Season: 2 PushMi Ups!
Rarity: Common
Scent: Choc Chunk
Dream Vacation: *Neigh*braska
Dislikes: **Night***mares*

Favorite TV Show: *So You Think You Can Prance*
Favorite Treat: Anything chocolate
Best Joke: What did the mare say to the foal? It's pasture bedtime!

Scoops

SO CUTE

Scoops the Mouse lives in an ice-cream-cone condo. When this Pikmi gets hungry, it simply eats a hole in the wall! You can never have enough windows, after all!

Animal: Mouse
Season: 2 PushMi Ups!
Rarity: Common
Scent: Mallow Mix
Favorite Treat: Marshmallow cheese sandwiches

Dislikes: Drips
Hobby: Riding the Ferr-swiss Wheel
Quote: "What's the scoop? I'm all ears!"

Icey

SO CUTE

As cool as ice and extra nice, Icey the Bunny is a popular pick on a hot day! Other Pikmis line up to cool down with a hug from this chill bunny!

Animal: Bunny
Season: 2 PushMi Ups!
Rarity: Common
Scent: Marshmallow Ripple
Likes: Hoppy endings
Looks Forward To: Trips to the *hare*dresser

Hobby: Ice sculpting
Favorite Dance: The bunny hop
Favorite Treat: Marshmallow ice blocks

Sorbae

BE HAPPY

Sorbae travels everywhere using bubble power! It's a very relaxing way to travel, but you have to make sure you can go with the blow!

Animal: Bear
Season: 2 PushMi Ups!
Rarity: Common
Scent: Bubblegum Swirl
Twin: Ollie
Known for: Going with the blow of things

Hobby: Bubblegum ballooning
Hero: Winnie the Pooh
Favorite Treat: Bubblegum sorbet

SWEET

Character Checklist

There are so many precious Pikmis to choose! Place a check mark next to the ones you have and collect them all!

Akwa	Dollop	Folly
Alfalfa	Dream	Freckle
Asha	Dreya	Fuwa
Bamboo	Drips	Fuzz
Beeps	Ebby	Gizmit
Bibble	Eggnog	Glama
Bobble	Erkle	Guggles
Brite	Fab	Hobnob
Bubbles	Fancy	Hoodoo
Chata	Fetti	Icey
Chomp	Fez	Ickle
Cloppy	Flit	Juju
Clove	Flubb	Kaz
Dainty	Fluff	Kazoo

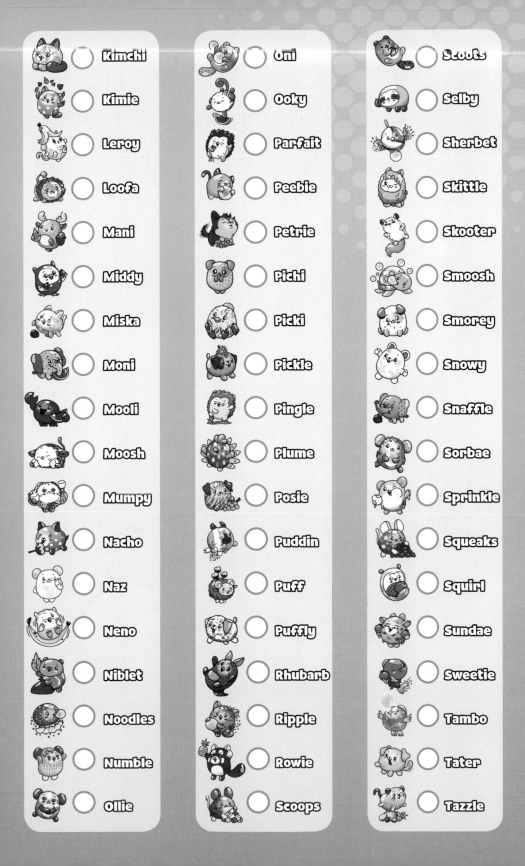

Kimchi	Oni	Scoots
Kimie	Ooky	Selby
Leroy	Parfait	Sherbet
Loofa	Peebie	Skittle
Mani	Petrie	Skooter
Middy	Pichi	Smoosh
Miska	Picki	Smorey
Moni	Pickle	Snowy
Mooli	Pingle	Snaffle
Moosh	Plume	Sorbae
Mumpy	Posie	Sprinkle
Nacho	Puddin	Squeaks
Naz	Puff	Squirl
Neno	Puffly	Sundae
Niblet	Rhubarb	Sweetie
Noodles	Ripple	Tambo
Numble	Rowie	Tater
Ollie	Scoops	Tazzle

Tickle

Tickles

Tiki

Toogy

Tubble

Tubbs

Tuku

Tumbles

Twigs

Twirl

Velvet

Voom

Wawa

Wisp

Wubbs

Zeni

BE HAPPY

SO CUTE

SWEET